Fasting For a Breakthrough

Bishop Herbert V. James

Fasting For a Breakthrough

Published by
Kingdom Kaught Publishing, LLC.
Denton, Maryland 21629 USA

Copyright © 2011 by Bishop Herbert V. James

All rights reserved. No part of this book may be reproduced or transmitted in any form or by any means without written permission of the author.

Unless otherwise indicated, all Scripture quotations are taken from the King James Version of the Bible.

Cover design by Agape Advertisement, Inc.

Interior design by Kingdom Kaught Publishing, LLC.

ISBN 978-0-9824550-1-2

Library of Congress Control Number (LCCN): 2011920015

Table of Contents

Introduction 1

What is Fasting? 5

Your Purpose for Fasting 11

Don't Get It Twisted 19

Just Not Eating 21

Isaiah's Fast 25

Fasting For the First Time 29

Back To Isaiah 33

Moses' Fast on Mount Sinai 37

The Ezra Fast 39

Esther's Fast 45

Daniel's Fast 49

Joel's Fast 53

What Would Jesus Do? 55

Cornelius' Fast 57

Fasting For a Breakthrough 59

Bibliography 61

Introduction

For hundreds of year's modern day Christians throughout the world and across every denomination talk about fasting. Some see fasting as simply not eating while others see fasting as a special time of meditation. Yet others see it as a special time of prayer and supplication. Each of these are true within their respective categories but is only a part of the whole fasting concept especially when you are looking for a breakthrough.

One day prior to a fasting period, a discussion arose as to what a person could or should eat during a fast. Who selects the foods or the absence of a special type of food within the menu of choices? This was an interesting question since nowadays Christians have sliced and diced fasting into segments of food groups; Fruit fast, meat fast and I have even heard of a cookie and candy fast. Fasting specific portions of food groups has never been the purpose of a fast. Fasting is not the limitation of a food group specifically but rather food completely! I am not saying that groups of foods can't be eliminated but the elimination of some type of food or where you're eating a full course meal except dessert is not a fast that will bring about the Lord's intervention. A true fast in terms of spiritual blessings and obtaining a breakthrough on a certain situation, problem or illness requires more than the absence of ice cream & cake. Don't laugh because although this may sound ridiculous, many people practice this type of fasting expecting God to move on their behalf. They eliminated certain types of foods and expect a miracle. This practice as you will soon see does nothing in bringing about a spiritual breakthrough.

Recently, my own church as it has in the past entered into a month long fast but for some reason this year, probably due to the growth and evolution of the body of Christ within my church, the question of a proper fast became loudly expressed. Questions range from, "I'm sick and must eat because of the medication I take, so what should I do?" Do I go by the ingredient of an item to determine if I can eat it during an Ezra Fast" and everything in between? Such questions and the lack of knowledge in this area despite the thousands of previously written books on the topic have urged me to write this little guide to Fasting for a Breakthrough. This guide actually complements a sermon series I ministered early in my ministry, and though that was years ago, it is just as viable today as it was when I first preached it. I certainly do not claim any authority within this subject but use the bible as my full

Introduction

and complete authority on the subject. This is a starter book for those new to fasting or those who have specific questions on fasting that might not have been answered previously and in some cases confirm something that the Lord has already spoken to you about the topic of fasting. Generally speaking, most people don't understand the fast or the need for it. This guide is primarily for the multitude within my geographical church body but is a valuable resource that should be used by any kingdom reader. The one thing that must be remembered is that the bible is true and the invaluable truth in its totality. Even though I understand that there are those who swear upon the New Testament and those who rely greatly on the Old Testament, many times we push aside the Old Testament writings for the New Testament writings because there are those who claim that the church walks in the period of Christ that begins with the New Testament. Although this is true, like with tithing, the blessings of God and other foundational realities such as fasting is as much an Old Testament reality as the new. Esther called the Jews to a fast, as did Ezra, Isaiah, and Daniel. Of course, a primary New Testament fasting scripture points to Jesus' 40 day fast and later the need for fasting during a really difficult situation when Jesus was forced to explain to his disciples that "this kind goeth not out but by prayer and fasting!" Certainly none of this can be overlooked or under emphasized. Jesus by bringing this important fact to our attention is pointing us back to the foundation of the Old Testament fast.

What is fasting? How is it accomplished? How is it combined with prayer and why is it needed since most people would argue that prayer has been proclaimed to be the way that God answers our situations? Fasting is a topic that is grossly misunderstood by many. Yet, irrespective of our knowledge, or the lack of it, there is a great deal of power found in the proper understanding of the fasting principle. Older saints and new comers alike sometime refuse to consider fasting for a multitude of reasons ranging from the lack of importance of fasting to the fear of getting sick or hungry from the lack of food. Although some of us could stand to actually skip a meal or two in our daily dietary routines for purely health reasons, fasting as you will find holds great importance and power in the life of the believer.

Chapter 1

What is Fasting?

Fasting is going without food or drink voluntarily for a specific or defined period of time so that during that time you can concentrate on God. Fasting according to Wikipedia Encyclopedia is primarily the act of willingly abstaining from some or all food, drink, or both for a period of time. The New Illustrated Bible Dictionary notes that generally fasting is for religious purposes, however fasting can also be done for other reasons. The Law of Moses specifically required fasting for only one occasion, the Day of Atonement. In fact, the Day of Atonement was called the day of fasting. It is more popularly known as the Jewish Holiday of Yom Kippur which is considered to be the most important day on the Jewish calendar. Fasting during Yom Kippur is so important that unless your health is placed in danger by fasting no one above their bar or bat mitzvah is exempt. Traditionally it is observed by a 25 hour period of fasting and prayer. In other cases, voluntary group fasts were entered into during times of war (Judges 20:26) (I Samuel 7:6). Jehoshaphat called for a fast when opposed by the Moabites and Ammonites (2 Chronicles. 20:3). A seven day fast was held when the bones of Saul and his sons were buried. In the New Testament we find that Cornelius was fasting at the time of his vision in Acts 10:30 for four days. The church at Antioch fasted and sent Paul on his missionary journey. I Corinthians 7:5 instruct married couples to abstain from sexual intercourse for a while to give themselves to fasting and prayer.

The word fasting from the Hebrew perspective when spoken of by Jesus in Matthew, Chapter 17 refers to self-denial. It begins as a natural expression of grief; it's when you are so upset that you just can't eat. You don't have a desire to eat, just sit and be still trying to figure out what to do next. It is in those times of loneness wondering what to do next that forces us not only to search ourselves but also to seek God. Everybody tends to seek God in times of trouble, so fasting became a basis for making one's petition known to God through self-denial, looking for what God is saying to us rather than what we are saying to Him. Moreover fasting is not limited to Christianity although this writing is based on it from a Christian viewpoint. For Roman Catholics, fasting consists of reducing one's intake of food to one full meal and that meal cannot contain meat during Fridays of the Lenten season. Eating solids between meals is not permitted and fasting is a requirement of all faithful Roman Catholics. Greek-Catholic

What is Fasting?

Christians and the Eastern Orthodox believers maintain that fasting is an important spiritual discipline, and according to sacred tradition fasting is to guard against gluttony and impure thoughts, deeds, and words. For members of the Church of Jesus Christ of Latter-day Saints, fasting is encouraged on the first Sunday of each month which is designated as Fast Sunday. Fasting for the Church of Jesus Christ of Latter-day Saints is total abstinence from food and drink. Thursday fasting is a common practice among the Hindus in Northern India as well as during religious festivals. If fasting is followed in its strictest form by the Hindus, no food or water is consumed from the previous day's sunset until 48 minutes after the next day's sunrise. Fasting for a month is an obligatory practice during the holy month of Ramadan in the Islamic religion. Muslims are prohibited from eating, drinking, smoking, or even engaging in sexual intercourse while fasting. From a health perspective fasting is natural for the day-to-day health of God's people and we actually fast regularly each and every day. Of course, our daily fast is for proper health not for spiritual insight. Every day we initiate a fast when we go to bed. We break that fast when we arise and have our first meal, whether cereal, bagels, or just coffee. That is where we get the word breakfast, because when you wake up in the morning and eat you are literally breaking your sleeping fast. Now you must understand that this natural daily sleeping fast is not a fast being used to seek God's face on some issue or situation. Let me say that again, this natural daily sleeping fast is not one that is being used to seek God's face on some issue or situation, this natural fast is set up by God for your physical health. Your night time (or sleeping fast) is important to your body's digestive function and over all health. That is why medical doctors advise you not to eat four hours before you plan to go to bed for the night. Whether your nighttime fast is during the day because of your work schedule, you are still not supposed to eat for four hours before you sleep for the day. This is so that when you lay down your internal system will not have to work hard digesting food. Your heart rate slows down, as does your breathing, and other internal body functions, i.e. kidneys, liver etc. It provides rest for the many cells that are present in your body and most importantly your digestive system. Your nighttime resting or sleeping fast helps to unclog your system and eliminate poisons. The many cells that are present in our body use this sleeping fast to process and eliminate waste throughout your body. Once you awake in the morning, your internal systems begin to pick up again and start working at full force. Thus, when you eat your first meal of the day, you are breaking your sleeping fast. As you can see, you have been practicing fasting since you've been born into this world and it has a serious purpose for your health. It has been shown in many empirical scientific studies that fasting improves health. I read a notation by Dr. Joel Fuhrman where he asserts that a true fast consists of an intake solely of water. He maintains that pure water can not only detoxify cells and rejuvenate organs but can actually cure such diseases and conditions as cardiovascular disease, rheumatoid arthritis, asthma, high blood pressure, type II diabetes, colitis, psoriasis, lupus and other autoimmune disorders when combined with a healthy diet. Studies have shown that fasting can lead to improved insulin and blood sugar control, and neuronal resistance to injury. Likewise, fasting has a serious purpose for your spiritual health as well. Self-denial should not be new to the born again believer since Jesus tells us that "if any man will come after Him, let him (or her) deny himself, or remove self-considerations, take up his cross, and follow Jesus!" Whisper, "Deny himself" so that this principle can get into your spirit. In the fasting process, denial is a physical manifestation that will open up a kingdom reality in your life and your life situation.

Chapter 2

Your Purpose for Fasting

As mentioned previously, there was only one fast appointed by the Mosaic Law in the Old Testament and that was on the Day of Atonement. According to Nelson's New Illustrated Bible Dictionary the following definition of the Day of Atonement is given; the tenth day of the seventh month was set aside as a day of public fasting and humiliation. On this day, the nation of Israel sought atonement for its sins (see Lev. 23:27; 16:29: Num 29:7). This day fell in the month equivalent to our August. This was a corporate public fasting and it was a full and complete fast. In Isaiah 58:6, God gives us one of the purposes for fasting. Here God says: "Is not this the fast that I have chosen to loose the bands of wickedness, to undo heavy burdens and to let the oppressed go free and that ye break every yoke!" We'll examine that text more, but as you can see, fasting is an important element in our battle with the powers of darkness. Wickedness, burdens, oppressions and bondage are the powers the devil wants to entrap us with. They are the powers of darkness. Let's look at Matthew 17; it is a powerful illustration that we need to see.

In Matthew 17, Jesus is approached by a man whose son was labeled as a lunatic and who was sore vexed. As a result of this boy's condition, the father explained that the boy would lose control of himself and fall into the fire, and sometimes into the water. These points are significant because it is the devil that walks around seeking whom he may devour, so let's take a few minutes and look at these two words. Vex according to Vine's Expository Dictionary means to disturb, to trouble, or to torment. A lunatic is referenced to the word "epileptic" that comes out of a root word that means "moon struck." That is because epilepsy was once thought of as being influenced by the moon. This man whose name is not mentioned specifically brought his son for help. He had no idea what his son's real problem was. Maybe it was a medical condition or simply some retardation. Nonetheless, the father felt that the church could help. Many times we miss diagnose our conditions in life and blame it on stress, on nerves, or on our jobs when in reality it is nothing more than the devil wreaking havoc in the life of the believer. Of course, that should not be anything new to the believer because the devil is looking for our weakest moments. He spends time analyzing you, trying to figure out the best way to get you! Remember, the devil looks for people that he may devour, not that he can devour them but he looks for those who have possibility.

Are you on his hit list? Is he going to try and devour you (even though he knows that he can't defeat you because you are God's child)? You are God's property and he cannot take what belongs to God. Glory to God! And yet, he is going to try. He has to try. That is his job and though he can't snatch you from the hand of God he can discourage you and hinder you. He can redirect you and get you off kilter, out of focus, and misdirected. He and his demons try to get you to think that there just may be something that is impossible for God to handle when the reality is nothing shall be impossible for God! Obviously this man knew that if he called on the elders of the church, his son could be healed from whatever troubled him. He brought his son to Jesus and asked Jesus to have mercy on his son. However, the real kicker is what the man says to Jesus next. He tells Jesus that he took his son to Jesus' disciples and they could not heal his son. These disciples should have been fully capable to handle the situation just as you should be able to today. What stopped them? Better yet, what's stopping you? This was a dispensation of time when the disciples were in the presence of Christ Jesus. According to the fourteenth chapter of the book of John, they should have been able to at least do what Jesus was able to do. In today's church, we should actually be doing greater works! Not more powerful but more diverse works because of the power of the gospel of Jesus Christ by the Holy Ghost. Yet some of us are doing things in the name of Jesus and getting absolutely no results. More important is that you can hurt yourself and confuse non-believers who are watching to see what Jesus is all about. There are those who think they have overcome a situation only to find that what they thought they had overcome, really overcame them.

In this encounter, Jesus quickly rebukes the devil that controlled the actions of the boy and the bible says that according to Jesus' command, the devil departed out of the child and the child was instantly healed. This led to a great discussion among the disciples because the disciples later came to Jesus in a private place to inquire why they couldn't cast the devil out of the boy themselves. It is here that Jesus takes the liberty to teach the disciples and us two powerful truths. First, Jesus says that they could not cast the devil out because of their unbelief, and secondly, because there are some things that won't go out without a combination of prayer and fasting! There are some things that prayer can handle alone but the tough stuff needs a combination of prayer and fasting. There are some situations in our lives that are so dramatic, so complex, so earth shattering that ordinary means have no effect. Remember, fasting places us into a position to hear what God is saying to us. We often hinder our prayer response because of our own personal issues and sin. We can actually stop God's response by our own actions.

Our own personal issues, if we are not careful, can hinder God's response to our issue. Either by the devil blocking your response or by you blocking your response. There is something called "besetting sins." The writer of Hebrews describes "besetting sins" as those sins which does so easily beset us. "Besetting sins" are not sins of neglect or momentary lapse of weakness. Most are generational based but the simplest and most devastating is a sometimes overlooked sin that followed you over from the days before you accepted Jesus Christ. You don't believe that the situation you have in front of you can be resolved by divine intervention because you don't look at the situation as being spiritual in nature. So as a result, you begin using your natural senses to attempt to handle it by natural means which in reality is a spiritual situation in your life. This can be dangerous since it prohibits the movement of God. Faith pleases God! Faith is paramount in the life of the believer since it is the very basis of Christian salvation. You must believe! If you confess with your mouth the Lord Jesus and believe in your heart that God raised him from the dead, you shall be saved (Romans 10:9). Confessions alone will not due it just as in some cases, prayer as powerful as it is, won't do it alone. Not because God isn't capable but because you aren't in a position to allow God to work in your situation.

Jesus makes it clear that "this kind" goeth not out but by prayer and fasting." If the person who is praying is not consecrated, then the result will be limited. The term "this kind" refers directly to demonic spirits, and Jesus says demonic attacks require this combination. Let me regress for a moment because you must first believe that there is such a thing as demonic spirits. Most modern day Christian's don't! Christians think that they are always in the flow and nothing can go wrong. When it does, they look only to what they can see, so most only see the person or situation and not the demonic force behind the actions of that person or situation. According to Vine's Complete Expository Dictionary a demon was signified among pagan Greeks, as an inferior deity whether that demon was bad or good. In the New Testament it denotes simply "an evil spirit." "Demons" are the spiritual agents acting in all idolatry. The idol itself is nothing but every idol has a "demon" associated with it that induces idolatrous acts. Demons disseminate errors among men, and seek to seduce believers to do wrong. From a much stronger position, people can be possessed of demons and not simply controlled by the direction of the demon. Those who are thus afflicted expressed the mind and consciousness of the "demon" or "demons" indwelling them. Demons do the bidding of the devil and since the devil knows he can't stop God, his focus is on messing with you so that you can't focus on what God has for you and the direction God wants you to take.

Chapter 3

Don't Get It Twisted

It's nice how Christians have labeled various fasts after the people who used fasting throughout the bible. I would love to have a fast named after me like some Christians have memorialized biblical people like Daniel, Ezra and others. Christians talk a lot about these monarchs of biblical history but as time has progressed, Christians have used the fasts of these monarchs as a title to support different types of fasting. However, let me make this perfectly clear once again, there is only one fast that these monarchs entered into. It was a total fast of no food.

These monarchs are noted by God throughout scripture to show us that fasts are useful during a variety of times in our lives. A fast is not just for one situation but for many situations. These various monarchs are not given for us to set up types of fasts but should be used as an example of situations where the fast can be used. Isaiah fasted at the command of God to loose strongholds, burdens, to release, and break yokes. Moses fasted for God's direction as did

Ezra and the list goes on. The need varies but the fast remained the constant.

There is only one fast! Don't get caught up in the view that there are types of fasts. Fasting is the absence of food for a period of time. To understand this we have to go back to the Law of Moses which required fasting on the Day of Atonement. It required that no food be eaten for a 25 hour period and everyone had to participate unless there was a major health risk. This is our guiding principle. Every fast, if it is to be called a spiritual fast is a no food fast. You'd better hear me! There is a reason God set this as a part of the Law of Moses and cannot be overlooked. God's fast and any fast that requires something of God is absent food intake.

These well-known fasts that everyone has adopted as entitlements simply show us the power that the fast has in various situations and should not be confused as types of fasts. There is only one type of fast and that is the absence of food. Now that is not to say that God cannot speak to you to and tell you to fast from a specific type of food. In that case, God is looking at your obedience and may have an underlying spiritual significance by God however absent God specifically speaking to you to change the pattern, a fast is the total absence of food.

Chapter 4

Just Not Eating

Fasting isn't, "just not eating." There is more to it than that! When you turn down your plate for a period of time, whether for one entire meal, a day or for any given length of time, that by itself is not what brings together the power needed to deal with what Jesus called "this kind," the demonic control or demonic suggestions of the devil. When you turn down your plate, this is time to be given to prayer, meditation, and the reading of God's Word so that the revelation of God can be revealed in your life and your situation. Your self-denial of food empties you to receive what God has in store to tell you. Not eating alone will not do you a bit of good, you can do that anytime. The business of the day or the thought of your problem can cause you not to eat but it's what you do during that time or period of not eating that can make the total difference in the spiritual battlefield. If all you are doing during the time you aren't eating is to further think about your personal problems or situation nothing will be accomplished. You will be in the same condition and hungry once you are done. However, if you take that same time and think about the promises of God and open yourself up to the direction God has for you through the indwelling Holy Spirit in your situation, suddenly you will notice that it isn't as bad as you first thought. True spiritual fasting opens portals for you and God to communicate. It takes your thoughts away from your problem and focuses on God's answer to your problem and you won't get hungry. Pressing into the presence of God and allowing Him to pour into you removes hunger. Hunger during the fasting process is a trick of the devil. Let me prove it. We go without eating all the time. Some of us skip lunch or breakfast or some other meal for some other reason but to do so is not fasting in the sense of obtaining a spiritual breakthrough for your situation. Don't cheat yourself out of your deliverance or breakthrough by telling yourself that you already skipped a certain meal and therefore you are already fasting because if you did not seek God you still have no spiritual direction or solution to your problem. If you are fasting for a spiritually divine breakthrough you cannot count meals you already missed routinely, that time has already passed. Therefore, that meal should not enter into your equation since it was not regularly there anyway and there is no self-denial and no meditation or communication with God. The meal that you do deny, or should I say the time period that you would be eating MUST be spent in meditation with God, seeking his face through reading of your bible, given to prayer, and most importantly personal soul searching for your deliverance and direction for your situation. Jesus said "this kind does not go out but by prayer and fasting." There MUST be the two "prayer & fasting" and it must be at the same time. It's a spiritual combination. A one-two punch! Fasting now and praying later is not going to bring a breakthrough! Prayer & Fasting is the required combination for difficult situations of "THIS KIND!" True fasting is supposed to bring you into the presence of God's glory. His Shekinah! The glory of God was exhibited in the character and acts of Christ in the days of His earthly ministry. It is God's manifested perfection of His character, especially His righteousness for which all men fall short. There are words that are commonly used in the church that are used simply because other people use them. They sound nice and religiously correct and when we repeat them it makes us sound like we know what we're talking about. Yet in reality, we have no clue and we're quick to say "Amen" or "praise the Lord." Using terms that you don't understand is dangerous. It's a true saying that our people perish due to the lack of knowledge. Take "Amen" for a moment. Amen is a declaration! When you say "Amen" you are declaring "so it is!" In other words, when you say "Amen" you are standing in agreement with whatever was said, you are declaring it to be absolutely true. Amen says that you are in agreement. That's why it is so important to know the bible and the promises God has for you. You need to know that there are guarantees that God has provided for his people who follow him through Christ Jesus. The promises of God are yes and amen.

Chapter 5

Isaiah's Fast

Earlier I made reference to Isaiah 58:6 which ask the question "Is this not the fast that I have chosen to lose the bands of wickedness, to undo the heavy burdens, and to let the oppressed go free, and that ye break every yoke?"

According to Isaiah 58, God provided a fast for four (4) areas of concentration:
1. To loose the bonds of wickedness
2. To undo heavy burdens
3. To let the oppressed go free, and
4. To break every yoke

These are the areas that this specific fast were setup to deal with and although set up into four groups of concentration, they cover far more as you will soon realize. Now remember that God set up this fast for a specific purpose and includes self-examination. Not for direction but rather for the illumination of our own spiritual position. A simple question to ask yourself is where are you now with God? Where do you want to be or deserve to be? Most of us, if we were honest would have to admit that we are not completely where we want to be in our relationship with God through Christ Jesus. Examine the area that this fast is set up to address and I ask you, do you have any of these situations in your life? I hear most of you saying that you don't have any of these situations and I pray you are being honest with yourself. But if you live long enough, at some point you will find yourself in one if not more of these categories.

1. bonds of wickedness
2. heavy burdens
3. oppression
4. yoke

Look at this closely, at the opening of Isaiah, Chapter 58, fasting was not getting the results that the people of God were looking for. Fasting simply wasn't working! Now I know this is a shock to most of you and probably an abomination in the eyes of my colleagues but don't think that because someone tells you to go on a fast or that you are asked to stand in agreement concerning a fast that the fast is automatically going to work. There are two sides to fasting, God's side and man's side. We want it to work and God says it will work, but there are things that are sometimes within ourselves and around us that will hinder us from achieving the breakthrough we seek. God's part is guaranteed because God is a perfect God. What isn't perfect, nor guaranteed is you! So you must do your part in the fasting process to examine yourself so that you do not hinder your own result. When we talked about the possessed boy in Matthew 17, we found that belief must be a part of the process. You must first believe. Remember everything of God is by believing. Your salvation is based upon it, so it makes perfect sense that belief be your starting point in the fasting process. Conversely, if you enter into a fast because you were forced into it, and you don't believe that it is going to work, it won't because your attitude won't support it. Likewise, if you resent having to fast, it won't work! It's like giving! The bible says that the Lord loves a cheerful giver. II Corinthians 9:7 says when talking about giving, that every man according as he purposeth in his heart, so let him give; not grudgingly, or of necessity, for God loveth a cheerful giver." If the purpose in your heart is wrong or if you are doing it grudgingly or out of necessity, your fast won't work either. Just like your giving won't work! (Look for my book on Giving for a Breakthrough) The children of God during that 58th chapter of Isaiah, wanted to know why the results of their fasting was not working in their situation and their prayers going yet unanswered. They were doing what they thought they were supposed to be doing. They read and studied the word and fellowshipped with the saints of God. Yet it appeared that their fasting was going unnoticed. It's because they were doing it to be seen! Fasting is a serious tool available to the believer for dealing with the devil and the stuff he tries to use to hinder our walk with God. It can not be used for a show of religious participation. Fasting is serious business! Is this not the fast that I (God) have chosen? Yes. If God chose it, it has God's resulting power associated with it! However, if you misuse it, God will not be mocked. Fasting is not done to show off or to prove a point. It's done to get a breakthrough.

Chapter 6

Fasting For the First Time

Before we get more specific about the Isaiah Fast or begin to talk about other fasts that are mentioned throughout the bible, I want to give you a few helpful hints for those who have never fasted before. The first thing to understand is that you can't simply wake up one morning and decide to fast when you have never fasted for a spiritual breakthrough before. Before beginning your fast, consider what you are fasting for. What are you attempting to achieve. What are you seeking from God in your life's situation? You don't want your thoughts to be all over the place. All of us have problems in one magnitude or another but when you are fasting you must prioritize your situation from what is the most urgent and important to the least. That is not to say that you will always be on the mark however at least you will have a starting point. God will adjust your thinking and direction during your time of fasting. He will illuminate things and show you things that will bring you more into focus; you just need a starting point. Once you have decided what you are asking of God in your situation, then you must decide what fasting program is best for you. Since this is new for you, I certainly don't expect you to go on a seven day fast. You must start appropriately as your body, physical condition and need dictates. Who knows, you might have to jump in with everything you've got on the first time out because the need is just that urgent but such determination must be met with common sense. Remember, fasting is going without food for a period of time, where you substitute that time for prayer, meditation, and communication with God. However, regardless of the urgency, as you prepare for your fast, begin days before by changing your daily food intake. Most of us are fast food junkies. That should change in preparation for your first fast. Eat natural foods and stay away from processed foods such as hamburgers found in most local fast food restaurants. In addition, start drinking plenty of water. Beginners must plan their fast so as not to get sick. This is also true with the elderly and the sickly. You will have to decide what meal you will sacrifice, what group of meals, or whether you will fast one day, or several days, all day, or just one specific meal of the day. Determining what you want God to do in your situation, may also help you to decide how long you want to fast. Remember, there are some things that will not go without prayer and fasting! The sacrificing of one meal is far less traumatic to the new comer than fasting for an entire 24 hour period yet sometimes your need will be great! So the quicker you can decide, the quicker you can have deliverance from your situation. Once you have decided the length of your fast, and whether your sacrifice will be one meal or all meals, you will have to begin your fast. I suggest that as a new comer, on that first day, whether a single meal or group of meals, your sacrifice should be replaced with drinking water or juice with no sweeteners during the absence of your meal, especially, if you are on medication or elderly. Listen to your body and if you begin to feel sick, go on and eat something. It won't do you any good, nor will it provide any witness to the power of fasting if you make yourself sick. You may have to adjust your fasting to a different time of the day, or a different meal and even adjust the length of your fast according to your health, fitness, age, and medications, if any. What you don't want to do is to discourage yourself by getting sick and lose the power of fasting because of doubt. The devil would love to discourage you in any way possible because he knows that fasting is a tool to reverse the devil's hold on your life. When you sacrifice a meal, remember the sacrifice is not that you simply didn't eat. Your power comes from substituting that mealtime with prayer, meditation, bible reading and consecration in the Word of God. You want to bring yourself into the presence of God for those 20 to 30 minutes you would have taken to sit and eat! This is the time for you to lay your situation, concern or problem before God, ask Him to search you, and allow Him to minister to you. Your entire focus is your fellowship with God. Feel His glory and presence in your situation and expect His direction. It is important not to exalt yourself or the fasting process. The exaltation is to be toward God the Father through Christ Jesus the Son, by the power of the Holy Spirit. That means that your fast is nothing to boast about. In Matthew, Chapter 6, Jesus said when you fast do not look somber as the hypocrites do, for they disfigure their faces to show men they are fasting. He says but when you fast put oil on your head and wash your face. In other words, take care of yourself that you appear not unto men to fast but unto your Father which is in secret because your Father which sees in secret shall reward you openly. You do not have to impress anyone or prove to anyone that you are fasting. Impression is not important when you need strength, deliverance, and power. When you empty yourself to God, God will fill you up with that which you need in the time you need it. He will let you see things about yourself and about others that you've never seen before. The prophet Isaiah declared that the simple external showing of a fast carries with it no power and is futile.

Chapter 7

Back To Isaiah

"Is this not the fast that I (God) have chosen to 1) loosen the bands of wickedness. The word wickedness equates to sinful, evil, mischievous, and vicious acts against God's people. The bands spoken of here relate to straps. That means that there are straps or belts of sin, evil, and mischievous acts that are fastened around you that must be released. God has chosen fasting as a key tool to loose them from you. There are things and people that are around you that are not only sinful, but evil and mischievous that God wants you to be released from. They are holding you back and holding you down from things you may not even be aware of. The second thing God attributes to this fast is the release of "heavy burdens." Heavy burdens are not just everyday stuff but rather things that are seriously weighing you down day by day, week by week, month by month, or maybe year by year. These are situations that relate to oppression and hardship whether mental or physical. These are heavy and keeping you from progressing in the way God intends for you. The third area of concern is the "oppressed." God wants the oppressed to go free or be free! Oppression literally means to exercise power over. That is exactly what the devil likes to try to do to the children of God, he likes to try to exercise control over them, to such a degree that they lose their position and power in God. So this fast includes freedom from oppression and the obvious result of oppression is lack of freedom. Finally, God says that this fast will loosen yokes! A yoke in the Greek is something that couples or ties two things together. It is something that ties you to all types of stuff. Some of us are yoked to negative emotional habits. Some of us are yoked to stuff that is unproductive or unequal in our walk with God. It is negative enslavement. As we have discovered, a fast is not simply going without food for a period of time whether it is one meal, several meals, a week, or a month. Fasting is a time when we can be prayerful and meditate on God and His word. It is a time of personal preparation. A time to come into the presence of God since coming to church does not always bring you into His presence. Did that alarm you? I certainly hope not! It will bring you into worship and praise, and into prayer but many times personal situations, problems, and circumstances sometimes keep you from entering into His presence. The fast breaks you free of attachments that have created situations, problems, and negative circumstances. There are certainly a number of fasts that are spoken of throughout the bible and not all fasting is done for the same purpose or to obtain the same result. A meat fast is a fast where one eliminates meat from their diet. This type of fast is more for the individual's health than for seeking God for a solution to a pressing issue. What if you don't eat meat for a month! Vegetarians do that everyday of every year. And what are you doing at the time you aren't eating meat? Are you praying and seeking God's face? Probably not! You're still sitting down at the table eating during the same normal time. You're just not eating any meat! Where is the power in that? Typically when the spirit of the Lord lays upon you to fast a specific type of food that fast is mainly for your edification. It's to show your obedience to God and may be for your personal health but not a fast that creates a breakthrough of "THIS KIND." Many of us fool ourselves when we fast a specific type of food group. We call it a fast to be used to accomplish a breakthrough but in reality it accomplishes nothing but obedience and personal edification. Fasting for a breakthrough means going without food, period! Not going without a specific food group. When Isaiah fasted according to God's will, God give several specific promises which we should look forward to as His children, precious promises for those who keep the fast that GOD HAS CHOSEN. Not what you have chosen or altered to your liking. According to Derek Prince in his book "How to Fast Sucessfully"[1] there are ten specific promises; Illumination or enlightenment, Healing or restoring to soundness quickly, Righteousness that goes before us and the Glory of the Lord (or his abundance) protecting our rear, Answered Prayer, Continual Guidance, Spiritual Satisfaction and Spiritual Refreshing, Generational blessings, and Restoration. Who wouldn't want these promised blessings? That is why fasting properly is so important if you want a breakthrough. Every fast that is used in the bible for a breakthrough is a total food fast!

Chapter 8

Moses' Fast on Mount Sinai

Let's look at Moses' fast on Mount Sinai. The bible says "and he was there with the Lord forty days and forty nights; he did neither eat bread, nor drink water..." This was a time where a specific ingredient was mentioned as being omitted from a person's diet for a specific period of time. When Moses went before God on Mount Sinai he was there for forty days and nights and scripture says that for those forty days and nights he did not eat bread or drink water. Christian's have taken this to mean that Moses didn't eat bread nor drink water but ate everything else. This is not true. Bread in this text is a metaphor that simply means the necessities for the sustenance of life. This is not a partial fast or a fast from a specific food group as some would suggest. Moses ate nothing for 40 days and nights which should not be surprising since he was in the presence of God! When you are in the presence of God, as Moses was here, there is no need for food. Going that long without food can only be accomplished when you are in the presence of God. The text also says that Moses drank no water. Water like the word bread as used here brings to light no prophetic enlightenment except to reiterate that when you come into the very presence of God, He who created you and knows all about you; it goes without saying that He can sustain you in the absence of natural foods and water. Those who would suggest that this is a "partial fast" do err in my opinion since a partial fast is not a true fast as subscribed by the Day of Atonement. However what I see here is fasting at its root! Moses was on Mount Sinai in the presence of God Himself. Moses had to empty himself before the Almighty God and depend upon almighty God to sustain and maintain him, and so he did. Man can only survive for a short period without bread and water however, if I may repeat myself, the thing that sustains you during your fast is God's presence. That is why it is very important that fasting is entered into properly. When you sacrifice food from a physical standpoint you must elevate your spiritual self to compensate. Moses had no need for food while sitting in the presence of God the creator of heaven and earth.

Chapter 9

The Ezra Fast

The Ezra fast, as it is called by many, is a fast that deals with self examination as well as looking for God's direction for His people. In the book of Ezra, Chapter 8, verse 21, Ezra announces, "Then I proclaimed a fast there, at the river Ahava that we might afflict ourselves before our God, to seek of Him a right way for US, OUR LITTLE ONES, and OUR SUBSTANCE." God instructed Moses in Exodus to tell the Egyptians to let God's people go. He also told Moses that he would send them to a land that was filled with both milk and honey. These two ingredients Milk & Honey indicates the best of what God has for his children. Yet, because of the overwhelming disobedience of the children of God, the land of promise, the land of provision failed to produce for seventy years. The land that had been previously filled with God's provision for His people lay desolate. The problem is that this was the land that God promised to be filled with milk and honey and God does not lie. The Promised Land was the land with provision that was specifically given to them by God himself but because of sin, the promise of God became a curse to those who were disobedient. As God began to lead

His people back to their promised place, Ezra proclaimed a fast so that they might seek God for proper direction. Between the place that they were and where they were going, there would certainly be traps and battles that had to be dealt with. Ezra led the people into a fast at the river of Ahava that they might seek of God for the right way for THEM, THEIR CHILDREN, and THEIR SUBSTANCE to be managed. They needed God's direction just as you do now. That is what led you into contemplating a fast or even reading this book. This fast provided not only direction for the adults, but the children, and their substance; food, belongings, and possessions. As with previous fasts, they did not simply refrain from a specific type of food or food group but food totally. There was no mention of a specific time frame in this instance but whether of one meal or several meals, this fast was called so that they would pray and meditate upon God for advice and direction. They needed to open themselves up to what God had to say to them for this time of their life. They knew, just as you know that they were God's children and required God's direction, not their own, in this situation. When you open yourself up through the sacrifice of a fast, God will provide you with marvelous direction not only for you but for your children and your possessions. It was after this fast that they realized that some serious things needed to change in their life. Let me repeat that, it was after this fast that they realized that some serious things needed to change in their lives. It becomes a poor testimony to be singing about the power of God and testifying about the power of God and not able to use the power of God in your life. Ezra notes: so we fasted and besought God for this; and he (God) was entreated of us." Ezra and the children of God needed God's protection as a multitude of defenseless people made their way across the wilderness so that they could return to the place of promise. They had to get back to where God wanted them to be in the first place, and so do you! This is important to understand, if you are to understand the fasting process. There are many of us who need to get where God wants us to be. He has given us the promise of His provision and we're moving in one direction when God wants us to be moving in another direction. I understand that there is a fear with moving from your present circumstance, situation, or condition to where you need to be in God for your life and your family, because to get there you may have to go seemingly against the grain or your understanding. You may have to go against what everyone else may think about you. Yet in the midst of it all, frankly you are tired of being here: no job, no life, and no future. You're tired of just hanging out with the boys or the girls. You have discovered that there is more to life than working and paying bills and you want to move from where you are and move to where God wants you to be. Our hindrance many times is that we tend to approach a problem with the traditional problem-solving mentality. We brainstorm all possible solutions then choose the most viable solution out of our own human wisdom. The problem with that is that God does not always choose to operate in what appears to be the only possible solution. In fact, God delights in making the impossible, possible because God is a God of impossibilities. The bible says, "So we fasted and entreated our God for this and HE ANSWERED OUR PRAYER." When Ezra says that they wanted "to seek of God the right way for us," that means that they wanted to seek a righteous and upright path. And in doing so, the bible says that God "entreated" them. Entreated as used here gets it's meaning from the Greek word "athar" which means "to burn incense in worship, to listen to a prayer, more specifically, a spontaneous petition to God who is waiting to listen." The children of God wanted to ask God for a righteous and upright way and God was waiting to listen! Isn't that something, God is waiting for our petition. He's waiting to hear from us. What becomes important here is that Ezra and the people of God didn't fast while they were traveling, nor did they try to resolve their problem before they fasted. Some of us fast at the wrong time or we fast far too late. We've got to understand that the timing of our fast is just as important as the mechanics of our fast. Fasting produces spiritual introspect as well as seeks spiritual direction. If you fast too late, the problem or situation will have grown far beyond what you thought the original problem was. By then, what you may have originally set in your mind for your fast may now need to change significantly. Many times, it makes you look into your own mind, heart and soul as to how you feel about yourself and your God. You have to ask yourself where you are in your walk with God. Am I really where God wants me to be? Spiritual examination makes you look not only at yourself but also at your surroundings. It forces you to ask yourself, why you are in this situation and come to the realization this is not what God meant for you. Why are you stressing out? Why are you sick when God already promised you health? God promises to give you the desires of your heart. Fasting causes personal spiritual confession. If you would be honest with yourself, you would have to conclude like Paul "I have a struggle within myself. For I know that within me (that is in my flesh) dwelleth no good thing. For the good that I would, I do not, but the evil which I would not do, that I do. I have to keep my body under control and bring it into subjection." In fact, some of you reading this book have come to the conclusion within your heart that you can not do this thing by yourself. You need God to clear up and clear out some things. You need God to intervene on your behalf. You need a breakthrough right now! Notice that when they followed the direction of God, as they left the river Ahava, the hand of God was with them and delivered them from the hand of the enemy that laid in wait. There are circumstances, situations, and problems that "laid in wait" for you as you travel from one level in God to another level in God or from one point in life to another point in life. Ezra's fast put a stop to those demons and devils that were hiding in the shadows to mess with them and deter them from their place in God! Fasting will do that for you too!

Chapter 10

Esther's Fast

Queen Esther called upon the power of fasting to help the Jewish nation residing in the capital city to demonstrate that they were relying on the grace of God to resolve their desperate situation. The problem was that when Prince Haman was elevated to his position of prince by King Ahasuerus, everybody was to bow and give reverence to Prince Haman because the king had so ordered it. However Mordecai did not bow nor give reverence to Prince Haman. Mordecai understood that there should be no other Gods before the one and only true God and this made Prince Haman angry! The Bible says that he turned to wrath. It reminds us of the three Hebrew boys who also refused to bow and give reverence to anyone but God and in that case, the wrath of the king was kindled to such a degree that he ordered them thrown into a hot oven. Yet because of their faith and obedience, God brought them out without the hair on their heads being singed, nor their clothing being burned! In fact, they didn't even smell smoky. They were in the furnace but God sealed them from even the smell of smoke. Now remember that word "wrath?" It's a word that means "to oppress, to be violent, to do violence to someone, to hurt, to over throw, to tear down or extreme wickedness." Prince Haman turned to wrath against the children of God and sort to destroy all the Jews who were found throughout the kingdom. Moreover, Prince Haman even convinced the king to pass a decree that whoever else destroyed the people of Mordecai, the Jews both young and old, little children and women, a reward of ten thousand talents of silver would be paid. Haman put a price on the head of God's children. When Mordecai perceived all that was done he asked for Esther's help. Esther's instruction to Mordecai was to go and gather all the Jews together and fast. This fast was specific. Esther asked of the Jews to neither eat nor drink for three nights and days. This was a corporate fast that was asked which was free from any food or drink for a specific period of time, three days! Esther sought God's mercy as she went before the king against the law set forth by the enemies of God's people. Esther needed favor and she obtained it through the fast. Many churches go on corporate fasts for various reasons. A corporate fast must be specific and for a specific purpose. It takes the obedience of all the people. Much like corporate prayer, everyone who knows the value of prayer should be praying. Likewise those who know the value of the fast should be fasting. Moreover the individuals involved in the corporate fast do not have the option of deciding how to fast or when to fast.

Esther's Fast

If the Lord places a fast upon the leadership, the fast should be specific, and for a specific time frame. Whatever the Lord so designates is what people who know the value of the fast, should do. Nothing more and nothing less, it's an act of obedience. That means if the fast is for three days of no food or drink, then the individual can not on their own decide to do otherwise or the fast is invalid for that individual. That's one less individual joining in the power of corporate unity. "The more the merrier" is the mandate for corporate fasting and corporate prayer. The result of Esther's corporate fast was that she found favor in the eyes of King Ahasuerus which led to the hanging of Haman on the very gallows that were built by Haman to hang Mordecai. What a powerful testimony to fasting.

Chapter 11

Daniel's Fast

Daniel was not a stranger to fasting as it would appear. However many people confuse Daniel's dietary choice in one instance identifying it as a fast when it was clearly not meant to be so. Rather it was an act of obedience to God. Many people consider the fact that Daniel ate vegetables in one instance as a partial fast which provides them with bases for the partial fast concept. I guess in some way, it is a partial fast having abstained from everything except vegetables but it was certainly not meant nor indicated as a fast and shouldn't be used as a basis for a breakthrough fast except where such dietary needs may be required for medical purposes during a fasting period. Daniel does not call his choice of eating vegetables a fast and neither was it meant for that purpose. Daniel was being obedient to God. Let's take a moment to examine Daniel Chapter 1. In brief, Daniel along with Hananiah, Mishael, and Azariah were captives under King Nebuchadnezzar. The King however had made abundant provisions for the captives. They were even given a portion of the King's food and wine. However as honorable as the food and wine from the King may have been, it did not conform to the requirements of the Mosaic Law. The food from the king was, among other things, sacrificed and offered to pagan gods before it was given to the King. This was against the Mosaic Law. Moreover, the Mosaic Law also did not permit "strong drink." Most Jews diluted wine with water, sometimes 10 to 1 but the King did not. Daniel asked if he could be excused from eating the King's food and drinking the King's wine. Needless to say, Daniel's request was denied since an unhealthy boy would do the King no good. However, the Lord God gave Daniel favor in the eyes of a prison guard. Daniel requested a ten day trial period where he and the other three would be given only vegetables and water and he told the guard that their appearance would be better than that of the other's who were eating from the King's diet. And so it was, after the 10 day trial, Danial, Hananiah, Mishael, and Azariah appeared healthier and as a result they were allowed to continue on a diet of vegetables. No fasting was mentioned as this was an act of obedience to God and clearly not intended as a fast. I am not suggesting as I mentioned that this could not be adopted into a fast if medical conditions required it, but to say that this is the Daniel Fast is misleading though I have seen many who have adopted it as a fast.

Daniel did conduct a fast in chapter 10. In that situation, Daniel needed an interpretation for a terrifying vision.

The text says that Daniel mourned for three full weeks and ate no pleasant bread, neither came flesh nor wine in his mouth, neither did he anoint himself at all, till three whole weeks were fulfilled. Here, Daniel mentions specifically abstinence from bread, meat, and wine. Most would take that to mean he took up eating vegetables and drinking only water, as he did before; however, I do not subscribe to this thought! This matter was too important, Daniel needed a breakthrough and I would suggest that although he does not mention vegetables in his list of items he refrained from everything. I believe he ate nothing and resorted only to water. He says "I ate no pleasant bread" the word "pleasant" as used in this passage of Scripture is the Hebrew, "Cha-mad" which means "desired!" Daniel ate no desired bread, flesh or wine! Nothing that would have been desired was eaten for three full weeks. In some manuscripts the word "desired" is replaced with "choice." Choice simply means to take for oneself. Thus, Daniel took nothing for himself during this three week period. Daniel had been praying about the rebuilding of Jerusalem and return of his people. Prophetically, this chapter was speaking about the end times. The seventy weeks of Daniel which points to the time of the tribulation period. Daniel was looking for understanding to the vision. After Daniel's time of fasting was over the vision of the Lord Jesus appeared before him. I don't want to get into the entire story of what occurred when the Lord appeared to Daniel except to say that he fell into a slumber and was lifted up in stages. What is more important is that he was assured that his prayer and time of fasting came up before the Lord from the very first day it was started. Yet it took twenty-one days for Daniel's answer and the reason that was given is that the devil tried to stop his answer in the spiritual realm. "Yet the Lord, in a theophanic appearance to Daniel, appeared at the proper time."

As with anytime the Lord appears in your situation, it is always on time. This is important because you shouldn't become discouraged when you don't see the result immediately. Your prayer and fasting was heard from the very first day. Demons tried to hinder your result in the spiritual realm but because a thousand years is but a day in the mind of God while you were still praying and fasting your answer was on the way. Although the demons slowed your answer, what they didn't know is that their interference was all part of the plan of God because when your answer came, it was at the right time.

Chapter 12

Joel's Fast

Here is a fast that did not make the headlines like others but this fast is just as important. The children of the Lord were facing punishment for their sins. Many times there are things that we contribute to the devil that are really caused by our own disobedience. The Lord God was not happy and allowed the Palmerworm, Locust, Cankerworm, and Caterpillar to eat away their provisions. There were more than eighty varieties of locust but only four specifically mentioned in the text. Joel chapter one, verse four says, "That which the palmerworm hasn't eaten up, the locust will eat. And whatever the locust hasn't eaten, the cankerworm will eat. And if the cankerworm doesn't eat it, the caterpillar will!" This was a unique plague which caused desolation to the children of God. Can you imagine that everything you received of the Lord began to be taken away? Eaten up one after the other until you had nothing? Verse 13 says, "Gird yourselves and lament ye priests: howl, ye ministers of the altar: come, lie all night in sackcloth, ye ministers of my God: for the meat offering and the drink offering is withholden from the house of your God." Joel then says, "Sanctify or set apart unto God, ye a fast. Call a solemn assembly, gather the elders and all the inhabitants of the land into the house (the church) of the Lord your God, and cry (pray) unto the Lord." This was a corporate fast that was to be called by the ministers. All the people were to "fast and pray." This is the kind of fast for "this kind" of trouble. It was a corporate fast for a corporate sin. Remember what we said about the devil and his demons. They are spiritual agents acting in all idolatry. Every sin has a demon associated with it that induces the act of sin. The people were to sanctify themselves and no one was exempt, not even the babies or the new mothers. By their obedience both in the fast, and in the prayer, and in setting themselves apart unto the Lord, the Lord said He would restore the years that the locust, cankerworm, caterpillar, and palmerworm had eaten away, even more than before because they will eat plenty and be satisfied! That is the power of the fast.

Chapter 13

What Would Jesus Do?

The Cliché that surfaced about a year ago is "What would Jesus do?" Certainly that is a valid question. Jesus used the fast Himself. When Jesus was tempted by the Devil after he was Baptized of John in Galilee, the book of Matthew records, "And when he had fasted forty days and forty nights he was afterward hungry." This was a full forty day fast similar to that of Moses' fast in the Mount of Sinai. After all, this was God, the Son! He was all God and all human as well. He needed this time of fasting for all He was to face in bringing salvation to mankind. After His fasting the bible says that He was hungry. It was then that the Devil tempted Jesus to turn stones into bread. The Devil used the fact that Jesus was hungry to tempt Him in this area of weakness. Notice what Jesus said "Man shall not live by bread alone, but by every word that proceedeth out of the mouth of God." The writings of Matthew simply say Jesus fasted for forty days and forty nights but it does not give us the magnitude of His fast. However, the book of Luke, Chapter 4, and verse two, provides us with a much better understanding of Jesus' fast. There we find Luke's words, "being forty days tempted of the devil. And in those days he DID EAT NOTHING: and when they were ended he afterward hungered." That let's us know that Jesus ate nothing! That is the bases for all breakthrough fasting, no food! Nothing! Jesus is our example, is he not?

Chapter 14

Cornelius' Fast

Let's quickly look at another New Testament fast. A centurion Jew named Cornelius who the bible says was a devout man and a man who feared God along with his household, who gave alms and prayed always, fasted for four days. At the conclusion of his fast and his prayer, (the breakthrough combination) the angel of the Lord stood before him and told him to seek out Simon Peter. And as a result of Peter's conversation with Cornelius, Cornelius was baptized in the Holy Spirit first and then by water. Water baptism is secondary to being baptized in the Holy Spirit. It is baptism in the Holy Spirit that places the believer into the body of Christ Jesus. Water baptism only demonstrates outwardly or publicly what has taken place within the individual personally.

Chapter 15

Fasting For a Breakthrough

In all these fasts, the fast was the same. It was total; no food fast. What differed was the length of the fast, the need underlying the fast, and the result of the fast. Thus, the children of God must resist the temptation of modifying or reducing the fast to the abstinence of specific food groups unless the Lord absolutely and specifically guides you in that manner. Then, of course, remember that something like that is for you to show your obedience. Otherwise, a fast whether individual or corporate is the abstinence of food totally and that time given to prayer, meditation, and the study of God's Word. That is the fast that is for what Jesus notes, "This kind goeth not forth but by prayer and fasting!" Don't allow anyone to tell you otherwise. If you really want to achieve results, don't cheat yourself. At the same time, those of you who are approaching the fast for the first time, you must use common sense in your fast. Prepare and plan your fast. Prepare yourself and plan what plate you will sacrifice, whether breakfast, lunch, or dinner. You also have to plan for whether this fast eliminates all meals whether for a day, two days, or three. Are you elderly or sick? This will change your plan a bit and you must also consider what you are asking the Lord to do on your behalf. Only you know your situation and the results you seek. Therefore, your individual need will help you decide how much sacrifice you need and how long your sacrifice will be. As I mentioned in the beginning, you may just have to jump in full force right from the start because your need is so great and so urgent! Remember fasting for a breakthrough requires that you abstain from food totally for a period of time and during that same period of time, pray, meditate on God, and read His word. You are using the time you would be eating food to eat the word of God and to communicate on a spiritual plane. Some people have been so in tune with God during a fast that they began to speak in other tongues. The one-two punch of prayer & fasting is powerful and will defeat the devil and his demons in any situation. Keep in mind, there are some things that prayer alone can handle. Yet there are some things that will not leave you alone without prayer & fasting.

Bibliography

1. Vines Expository Dictionary by Vine, Unger, White 1985 Nelson Publishers
2. How to Fast Successfully by Derek Prince. Whitaker House 1976
3. The Bible Knowledge Commentary by John F. Walvoored & Roy B. Zuck, Victor Books 1985

About the Author

Bishop Herbert Vasco James is the 9th pastor of the Greater Holy Trinity Baptist Church, one of the historical black Baptist churches in Atlantic City. Bishop James, who was appointed to the pastorate in March 1994, quickly forged a new path for the ministry of the Greater Holy Trinity Baptist Church while holding onto the strong values of the church reminiscent of the 1950s under the leadership of the late Rev. Dr. John Jasper Walters. Bishop James was brought up and baptized in the Shiloh Baptist Church under the pastorate of the late Rev. Thomas O. Mills and served at three local churches after being licensed as a minister of the gospel; Mount Zion Baptist under the pastoral leadership of the late Reverend Robert Ellington and later Rev. Dr. Winfred J. Sanders, Calvary Baptist Church under the Pastoral leadership of Reverend Thomas B. Whitfield, and the Second Baptist Church under the pastoral leadership of the late Rev. Dr. Issac S. Cole. Bishop James was ordained by the Middlesex Central Baptist Association and by the International Ministerial Fellowship. Bishop H.V. James was elevated to the Episcopal Office of Bishop on Sunday, August 10, 1997 in the Abundant Harvest Fellowship of Churches where Bishop David G. Evans of the Bethany Baptist Church of Lindenwold is prelate. Bishop James is the former Southern N.J. Jurisdictional Bishop of the Abundant Harvest Fellowship. He is past secretary and past Vice President of the Fellowship of Churches of Atlantic City and Vicinity. He was a former member of the Board of Directors of the Garden State Bible School where he also sat as registrar.

In addition to his ministry, Bishop James is a retired Sergeant of police with 27 years of policing experience with the Atlantic City Police Department. Within those twenty-four years has amassed a wide array of certifications, accommodations, and citations.

www.ingramcontent.com/pod-product-compliance
Lightning Source LLC
Chambersburg PA
CBHW032017290426
44109CB00013B/693